Big
Science Ideas

What is pollination?

Bobbie Kalman
Crabtree Publishing Company
www.crabtreebooks.com

Big Science Ideas

Created by Bobbie Kalman

Dedicated by Katherine Berti
To my mom for the countless flowers with which she fills our gardens,
and to my dad for his guidance and inspiration in beekeeping.

**Author and
Editor-in-Chief**
Bobbie Kalman

Editor
Kathy Middleton

Proofreader
Crystal Sikkens

Design
Bobbie Kalman
Katherine Berti

**Production coordinator
and Prepress technician**
Katherine Berti

Photo research
Bobbie Kalman

Illustrations
Barbara Bedell: pages 6, 7
Katherine Berti: page 27

Photographs
iStockPhoto: pages 11 (bottom left), 26
Otto Rogge Photography: page 20 (top)
Other photographs by Shutterstock

Library and Archives Canada Cataloguing in Publication

Kalman, Bobbie, 1947-
     What is pollination? / Bobbie Kalman.

(Big science ideas)
Includes index.
Issued also in an electronic format.
ISBN 978-0-7787-3286-0 (bound).--ISBN 978-0-7787-3306-5 (pbk.)

     1. Pollination--Juvenile literature. I. Title. II. Series: Kalman, Bobbie,
1947- .Big science ideas.

QK926.K34 2011   j571.8'642   C2010-903014-1

Library of Congress Cataloging-in-Publication Data

Kalman, Bobbie.
  What is pollination? / Bobbie Kalman.
     p. cm. -- (Big science ideas)
  Includes index.
  ISBN 978-0-7787-3286-0 (reinforced lib. bdg. : alk. paper) --
ISBN 978-0-7787-3306-5 (pbk. : alk. paper) -- ISBN 978-1-4271-9440-4
(electronic (pdf))
  1. Pollination--Juvenile literature. 2. Pollen--Juvenile literature.
3. Pollinators--Juvenile literature. I. Title. II. Series.

  QK926.K35 2010
  571.8'642--dc22
                                                                    2010018040

Crabtree Publishing Company

Printed in Canada/052018/MA20180403

www.crabtreebooks.com   1-800-387-7650
Copyright © **2011 CRABTREE PUBLISHING COMPANY**. All rights reserved. No part of this publication may be reproduced, stored in a
retrieval system or be transmitted in any form or by any means, electronic, mechanical, photocopying, recording, or otherwise, without the prior
written permission of Crabtree Publishing Company. In Canada: We acknowledge the financial support of the Government of Canada through the
Canada Book Fund for our publishing activities.

**Published in Canada
Crabtree Publishing**
616 Welland Ave.
St. Catharines, Ontario
L2M 5V6

**Published in the United States
Crabtree Publishing**
PMB 59051
350 Fifth Avenue, 59th Floor
New York, New York 10118

**Published in the United Kingdom
Crabtree Publishing**
Maritime House
Basin Road North, Hove
BN41 1WR

**Published in Australia
Crabtree Publishing**
3 Charles Street
Coburg North
VIC, 3058

Contents

What is pollen?

Pollen is the yellow, white, or brown powder at the center of most flowers. Pollen is an important food for bees and some other animals.

The bee on the left is covered in pollen. Bees collect pollen in pollen sacs.

pollen
sac

An important part of flowers

Pollen is a very important part of many flowers. It is the part of a flower that plants need to make fruit, seeds, and new plants. To make new plants, pollen has to move from one flower part to another of the same kind of flower. Most flowers need **pollinators** to move their pollen. Pollinators are animals such as bees, wasps, butterflies, and other small animals that visit flowers.

This beetle has pollen all over its body. When it goes to another flower of the same kind, it will leave pollen on that flower. The flower will then be able to make seeds.

5

What is pollination?

Some flowers have male and female parts. The **stamen** is the male part of the plant that makes pollen. Some flowers have one stamen, and others have many. The **pistil** is the female part of the flower. It is made up of the **style**, **stigma**, and **ovary**. The stigma is the top part. It receives the pollen. The style is the pollen tube. The pollen travels down through the style to the ovary. The ovary contains **ovules**.

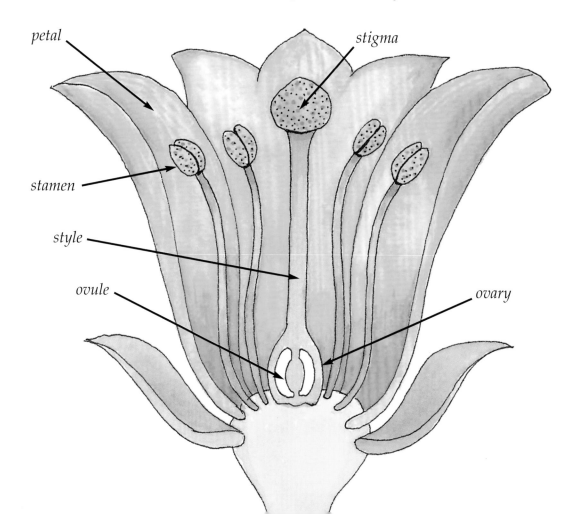

How a plant grows

When pollen moves from a stamen to a stigma, **pollination** has taken place. After a flower is pollinated, its petals fall off. The ovaries of the flowers become fruit, and the ovules become seeds. The fruit of a plant can be a vegetable or nut, as well as fruit. The fruit of the bean plant below are the bean pods. The seeds are the beans inside the pods.

Bees are pollinating the flowers of a bean plant.

After pollination, the ovaries of the flowers become bean pods.

The beans inside are the seeds that can make new plants.

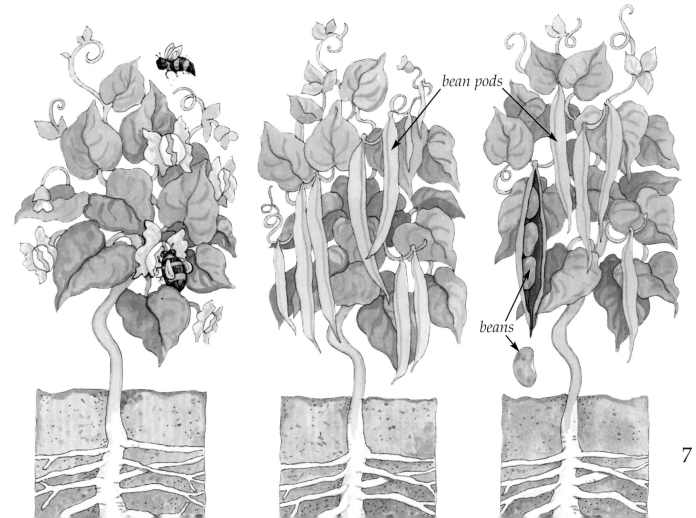

bean pods

beans

Types of pollination

Flowers cannot make seeds unless they are pollinated. There are three main types of pollination: **cross-pollination**, **self-pollination**, and **wind pollination**. In cross-pollination, flowers need pollen from other flowers of the same **species**, or type, to land on their pistils. Animals such as insects and birds carry pollen from flower to flower.

This bee is cross-pollinating. It is carrying pollen from one flower to another of the same kind.

Self-pollination

During self-pollination, pollen moves from the stamen to the pistil of the same flower. Flowers that self-pollinate have male and female parts that are close together, so the pollen can move easily from the stamen to the pistil. Sunflowers can self-pollinate or be cross-pollinated.

sunflower

ragweed

Wind pollination

Some flowers are pollinated by the wind. Wind sweeps pollen off those flowers and carries it to other flowers. Wind-pollinated flowers have millions of tiny pollen grains. These flowers seldom have nectar. Ragweed flowers are wind pollinated. Many people are very **allergic** to ragweed pollen.

9

Shapes and colors

Most animals pollinate when they look for **nectar**. Nectar is a liquid found in many flowers. The bright colors and sweet smell of a flower tells pollinators that the flower contains nectar or pollen for them to eat. Flowers that are pollinated at night have very strong **scents** to make it easier for pollinators to find them.

The luna moth is a beautiful nighttime pollinator.

Orchids have special markings that guide insects to their nectar.

A paper kite butterfly is pollinating an orchid.

The jack-in-the-pulpit plant does not smell sweet. In fact, it smells like dead meat. This plant attracts flies to pollinate it.

Hummingbirds have long beaks and very long tongues. They are able to feed at flowers that are too deep or thin for other pollinators to reach.

11

Do we need pollinators?

Did you know that more than one-third of the food you eat depends on pollinators? Pollinators make plants healthier so they can make a lot of food. There are thousands of kinds of pollinators. Most vegetables, fruits, and nuts come from plants that were pollinated by insects, birds, bats, and other small animals.

cherries

apples and pears

blueberries

All these foods!

The foods shown on this page, and many more, came from plants that were pollinated by insects and other animals.

kiwi fruit

all kinds of nuts

raspberries

chocolate and hazelnuts

many kinds of vegetables

13

Insect pollinators

There are thousands of kinds of insects that pollinate plants. They belong to five main groups: bees, wasps, butterflies and moths, flies, and beetles. Without these insects, we would not have many of the foods we eat.

bees

wasps

moth

butterfly

beetles

flies

15

Bees are best!

There are thousands of kinds of bees, but the honeybee is the most important pollinator. Honeybees are **social** insects. Social insects live together in groups called **colonies**. Each bee colony lives in a **hive**, which is its home. Bees collect nectar and pollen from flowers. They pollinate many kinds of fruit trees, as well as vegetable plants. They also make honey, which people eat.

bee on apple tree

Bumblebees

The bumblebee is another kind of bee pollinator. There are about 250 species of bumblebees. Bumblebees have big furry bodies. Like honeybees, these bees live in colonies of 150 to 200 bees. Bumblebees make their nests underground. The tongues of some bumblebees are short, and others are long. The long-tongued bees are important pollinators of many plants, such as beans, tomatoes, and clover.

Butterflies and moths

Butterflies and moths have long **proboscises**, or mouthparts, which can reach the nectar and pollen inside flowers. Butterflies like bright pink, blue, and purple flowers. Some moths are good pollinators of flowers that bloom at night. They look for pale flowers with strong scents.

The hummingbird moth can pollinate flowers that are too thin and deep for other pollinators. Its long proboscis can reach the pollen deep inside them.

proboscis

This butterfly has landed on a pink flower. It is using its long proboscis to sip the nectar. Its legs are covered with pollen.

proboscis

19

Wasps and flies

Wasps are mainly **carnivores**. Carnivores eat other animals. Wasps hunt small insects. Many insects live on plants. Wasps visit flowers to look for smaller insects that they can find there. They also drink flower nectar to give them the energy to hunt insects. While they hunt insects, wasps pollinate plants by carrying pollen on their bodies from flower to flower. Wasps also help nature by eating many insects that damage plants.

hover fly

Pretending to sting

Flies are very important pollinators because there are so many of them. The most important fly pollinators are hover flies and bee flies, but many other flies also visit flowers to feed on nectar. Hover flies have yellow and black stripes, but they are not related to bees or wasps. The flies, which cannot sting, pretend to be stinging insects to keep other animals from eating them.

Beetle pollinators

Beetles visit flowers for many reasons. Some eat the pollen and nectar in flowers, and some eat the whole flowers. Other beetles feed on the smaller insects that visit flowers.

Smooth or hairy?

Beetles that are smooth are not the best pollinators because pollen slides off their bodies. The best beetle pollinators are those with hairy bodies because the pollen sticks to their hairs as they travel from flower to flower.

(above) Ladybugs are beetles that feed on small pests, such as aphids. Aphids damage plants.
(below) Ladybugs also drink some nectar as a snack to give them energy.

Bird pollinators

There are more than 2,000 kinds of birds around the world that feed on nectar or on insects found in flowers. Birds are important pollinators. In North America, hummingbirds pollinate many kinds of wildflowers, especially those with trumpet shapes. Honeyeaters are pollinators in Australia and on many islands in the Pacific Ocean. Honeycreepers pollinate wildflowers in Mexico and South America.

When a hummingbird puts its long beak into a flower to drink the nectar, sticky pollen grains cling to its beak. Some of the pollen grains are then left at the next flower it visits. Hummingbirds have very good eyes and are attracted to red flowers.

Both the red-legged honeycreeper (above) and the green honeycreeper (below) have curved bills that can reach inside flowers to eat nectar and catch insects. The green honeycreeper likes to eat fruit. These birds live in Mexico, South America, and the Caribbean.

Many Australian flowers, such as this red hot poker, are pollinated by honeyeaters. The flower is a kind of lily.

25

Lizards, bats, possums

Animals that hunt insects often pollinate plants. Small lizards visit flowers to find insects to eat. When they visit a flower, pollen sticks to their bodies. Other animal pollinators include fruit bats and honey possums. Both eat nectar and pollen.

The honey possum is one of the few **mammals** that eats mainly nectar and pollen. Its long snout and tongue reach the nectar and pollen inside flowers.

Besides eating fruit, fruit bats visit flowers in the dark to eat nectar and pollen.

This green anole is looking for insects on these pink flowers.

Pollinators in danger!

Pollinators are very important to us. Without them, we would not have fruits, vegetables, nuts, honey, or chocolate. These important animals are disappearing from Earth. When people build in **wilderness** areas, animals lose their homes and their food. **Pesticides** and **diseases** are also killing many pollinating insects. As we lose our pollinating insects, we also lose our food supply. One of the most important pollinators, honeybees, are disappearing, and no one really knows why.

Fewer bees

Each year, there are fewer honeybees. The use of pesticides has killed many bees. Bees are also being killed off by two types of **mites** that have moved into honeybee hives. The bee on the right has mites on its body.

mite

mite

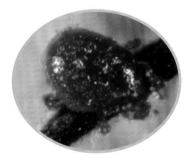

The Varroa mite attaches itself to a bee and feeds on fluids from the bee's body. The bee on the right has been treated for mites with powdered sugar. The sugar causes the mites to fall off the bees.

Helping pollinators

The best way to help pollinators is by telling everyone about why they are so important to us. Most people may think that bees, wasps, flies, beetles, and moths are pests. You and your friends can design posters to hang in your school and community to let people know that our food supply depends on these helpful animals. What other ways can you help?

*You can ask your parents to grow **native** flowers around your home. Pollinators need flowers!*

Thank you, pollinators!

Each time you bite into an apple, pear, or vegetable, say a silent "thank you" to the pollinators that made it possible. Count the number of times you say "thanks" in a day, and you will see just how important pollinators are to you and to everyone who eats!

Plant a vegetable garden. If you do not have a yard, you can plant vegetables in pots on a balcony. Bees and butterflies will love them, and you will love eating the delicious and healthy fresh foods.

Glossary

Note: Some boldfaced words are defined where they appear in the book.

allergic Describing a person who reacts negatively to a substance such as dust, pollen, or certain foods

carnivore An animal that eats other animals

disease Something that makes a living thing sick

hive The home of a bee colony

mammal A warm-blooded animal that gives birth to live young

mite A small animal that lives and feeds off other animals or plants

native An animal or plant that is found in a certain place or area

nectar A sweet liquid found in flowers

pesticide A chemical sprayed on plants to kill insects

pollen A powdery substance found in flowers that is needed to make fruit, seeds, and new plants

scent A pleasant smell

species A group of related living things that can have babies together

wilderness A place in nature where no people live

Index